THE IPAD PRO FOR SENIORS

A RIDICULOUSLY SIMPLE GUIDE TO THE NEXT GENERATION OF IPAD AND IOS 12

BRIAN NORMAN

Ridiculously Simple Press
ANAHEIM, CALIFORNIA

Contents

i

INTRODUCTION

The iPad does everything...but what if you don't want to do everything?! Sure, it's great that you can log into a private network or set up an iMAP / POP email account--but what if you are retired and just want to know the basics--like how to do a group Facetime with all the grandkids!

This book walks you through what you need to know step-by-step--including how navigation works now that the Home button is gone on some of the iPad Pros. It covers only what you need to know-- so you don't have to comb through hundreds of pages of tech-speak just to find out how to do a common feature.

This book is based on the bestselling book "The Ridiculously Simple Guide to the Next Generation iPad Pro" but includes sections specifically for seniors (including accessibility features that make text easier to see).

Are you ready to start enjoying your new iPad Pro? Then let's get started!

[1]

WAIT! WHERE'S THE HOME BUTTON?!

This chapter will cover:
- What's in (isn't) in the box
- The iPads buttons
- What's Face ID
- What are the new features to iOS 12
- How to use the iPad Pro when it doesn't have a physical Home button

WHAT ISN'T IN THE BOX

I don't usually cover what's in the box for product guides. It just seems like filler space and the point of this book is to just tell you what you absolutely need to know.

In the case of the iPad, what's in the box isn't as important as what isn't in the box. Sorry for the double negative, but this really is important.

What isn't in the box? Two things:

1. Lightning Adaptor
2. Headphones

Let's talk about the adaptor first because it ties into headphones.

I know, I know, I know--another adaptor, right?!

Apple has decided to move away from the Lightning port, which had been the method for charging iPads and iPhones for years, to USB-C. USB-C sounds like those USB drives but with a C stuck to the end; so, what's the difference? Cosmetically, USB-C is smaller (about half the size) and reversible (meaning there is no right side up when you insert it into your device).

So, Apple is doing all of this because it's smaller? Not quite! USB-C has three big selling points:

It's faster than regular USB

More power can go through it--enough to charge a laptop (or iPad in this case)

It's universal

At first glance, it's easy to look at that adaptor and see it as a torn in your side of endless cords but read that last part again: "It's universal." What does that mean? It means one day soon all device will use USB-C and you can share the cord. So, there will be no more digging in drawers for the right cable.

So yeah, a little annoying that there's another cable, but bear with them because USB-C is really progressing towards a less cord future.

Ok, so the headphones, or lack thereof. What gives?! Apple can literally put a 1 terabyte hard drive into this slim little tablet, but they can't fit in something as simple as a headphone jack?

I can't speak to Apple's design and limits, but the future of Apple devices seems to point fewer cords and clutter. That means using Bluetooth headphones.

If you still want traditional wired headphones, you have two options:

1. Buy USB-C headphones. They start for less than $10 and will get cheaper as

more people adopt USB-C and it be-
comes standard.
2. Buy an adaptor. These are also less than
$10.

TOUR THE HARDWARE

So, the real elephant in the room with the newest generation iPad Pro is the Home button or lack
thereof. In the next chapter, I'll talk about getting
set up, so I know this all sounds a little backward,
but because so many people are upgrading to the
new iPad Pro from an earlier model that had a
Home button, it's worth talking about the main
things that will be different about it here.

If you have used the iPad before, then I bet
you'll spend a good day continuously putting your
thumb where the button used to be! Don't worry!
You're going to get through it. In fact, after you
get used to it not being there, you'll actually start
seeing it's more effective without it.

Whatsmore, the missing Home button is be-
coming a standard feature on iPhones too; so, if
you will be upgrading to a Home-less iPhone soon,
then you'll be ready for it because it essentially
works the same way on the iPad.

Before diving into the gestures, let's cover
some other things that look different about this
iPad Pro.

The top portion of the iPad Pro looks like a
black bar, right? Look closer. A little more. More.

See it? There are cameras there. They kind of camouflage into the black, right? It's just the old fashion front-facing selfie camera, right? Yes, but there's more. There's a Dot projector, infared camera, flood illuminator. They all sound fancy, don't they? Fancy is...well fancy! But what on Earth does that mean in simple terms? It means that the front-facing 7MP camera can take pretty impressive selfies! But all those things also give you what you need for Face ID (which lets you unlock the iPad without the finger sensor you had on previous devices).

Okay, so all that's interesting, right? But you don't actually do anything with the sensors. What about the buttons on the tablet itself. Good question! Thanks for asking!

The button placement isn't too far off from previous iPads.

In the upper right corner, you have three things of note:

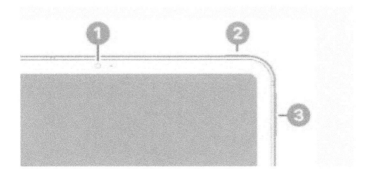

1. The front-facing camera (7MP)

2. The top button, which powers your device on and off, and puts it in standby.
3. The volume button

Turn the device over and on the right (right assuming the device is turn around) and you have a few more things of note:

4. The back camera (12MP)
5. Flash
6. Smart Connector (this is how the Apple keyboard, which is sold separately, connects to the iPad)
7. USB-C (where you charge the iPad)
8. SIM Tray (you will only have this if your iPad has cellular)
9. Magnetic connector (this is where you connect the Apple Pencil, sold separately)

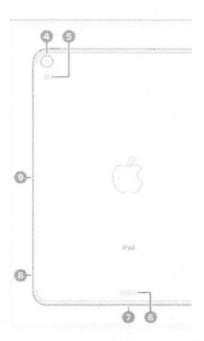

The appropriately named "Top Button" is more then a power button. Maybe that's why it's not called the Power button? Hmm. So, what is it?

The Top Button the button you use to power the iPad on and off--or to put it in standby (which is the mode you put it in after you finish playing Angry Birds in the bathroom and need to set the tablet down for a minute to wash your hands).

The most common use for the Top Button is to wake up your tablet. Picking up your iPad Pro and staring at it with an annoyed or confused expression will also do this. But if you ever find yourself stuck and picking up the tablet isn't waking it up, then just push down on the Top Button and you should be just fine. You can also tap the screen to wake it up.

If you are still on the fence about the iPad Pro and are reading this book just to learn more about it, then it's worth mentioning the actual feel of the device--or rather showing you a few pictures.

The most important picture is the one of the back camera. Take a look at it below. See how it pops out?

Why does that matter? To me it doesn't. But if you are an artist using the device on a flat surface, it's going to give it an unevenness. This can be solved by putting it in a case.

The next photos show the edges and thinness of the device.

THE APPLE KEYBOARD AND APPLE PENCIL

You may have bought the iPad Pro but haven't made you mind up about the keyboard and pencil. So, let's talk about both of those things briefly.

The Keyboard is well: a keyboard! But if you've had the old Apple keyboard case, then one thing you'll probably be happy about is that old origami style is gone; maybe it's just me, but I always had a hard time figuring out how to fold it! This only is much simpler.

Simpler means one position is gone; on the previous version, it could be used as a stand without the keyboard. Not the case anymore. It, of course, stands up with the keyboard open.

It also has two positions, so you can have two viewing angles; this is helpful when you are typing on your lap, but not as functional as keyboard case with more limitless possibilities with the position.

It's not terribly heavy, but it does add some weight; I recommend testing it at a store before buying.

Below are a few photos to give you a feel for what it looks like.

iPad Pro

Next, the Apple Pencil; I'll cover this more later in the book, but I do want to point out that the Pencil is pretty basic for this generation. It's completely redesigned, and it no longer comes with "tips. You have to buy those extra. They're pretty cheap though.

The biggest advantage of the new Apple Pencil is you don't have to plug it in. The previous generation had to be charged at the bottom of the iPad in the charging port, which really could get in the way. This generation is all magnetic.

FACE ID

Things were going okay with you and the Home button. You could rub your thumb over it and like a genie in a bottle, it would magically read your DNA and turn on. Why'd Apple have to go a ruin a good thing?

Sure, getting rid of the button gives you more screen real estate, but plenty of other tablets have added a button to the back of the device so you can have the both of both worlds. It's like Apple is trying to force you to love it, isn't it? I don't know why Apple does everything, but if past history teaches us anything, we have learned that Apple makes us adopt to better things by taking away the things we love. We loved our CD drives...and Apple took them out and put USB drives in their place; we got through it, though didn't we?! They did it again with the headphone jack. And on the iPad Pro and new Macbook's, USB is gone and, in its place, the faster USB-C.

Change is never fun, but it's not necessarily a bad thing. If you like numbers, you'll love this one. That little finger scanner has a ratio of 50,000:1-- that's the ratio of how hard it would be for someone to break into your iPad Pro. The iPad Pro with Face ID? 1,000,000:1. So if you're a fan of security, then Face ID is a no brainer.

If you're that person who is always throwing "What if" into the equation (you're the same person who morbidly asked, what if someone stole my tablet and cut off my finger to unlock it? Would the fingerprint scanner still work?), then I'm sure you have a few questions. Like:

What if I wear glasses and then take them off or put in contacts?

What if I have a beard and shave it? What if I think I look like Brad Pitt, but the iPad Pro says I'm more of a Lyle Lovett?

Sorry, Lyle, not everyone can be a Brad--but you don't have to worry about those first two points. Face ID has adaptive recognition, so you'll be just fine if you decide to grow it out for November. If you're in a dark room, Face ID will also still work--albeit with a little bit of help from the light sensor--which is a little annoying if your lying in bed and the only way to unlock your iPad Pro is to have a light turn on to scan your face--it should be noted, however, that it is pretty good at scanning faces in dark settings. If you're in a dark room, you can also just press that side button to open it manually and skip Face ID.

FEATURE THIS...

Every year, Apple dazzles us with dozens of new features. A lot of these features are under the hood, and don't sound very exciting, but they are making your iPad Pro perform better. Briefly, here are a few things people are excited about. I'll cover where to find these (and more) as I walk you around the iPad Pro and show you where things are.

Facetime with multiple people (up to 32 to be exact); this is basically Apple's way to combat Google Hangouts and Skype. Unfortunately, the feature is coming later in the Fall.

Animoji - This cute app lets you animate yourself; it was introduced with the iPhone X, but updated for the newest iOS.

Add stickers and filters when you are on FaceTime or when you take a picture in iMessage.

Screen time - The greatest and most depressing feature of the new iOS! This app tells us exactly how long we're using our devices.

Control your Notifications - With the newest iOS, notifications are grouped together (so if you have 40 emails and 10 text, it will show only one and when you press it, you can see what's stacked under it); you can also control how notifications are delivered--if you want them sent quietly, for example (you get the notification in Notification Center, but not on the lock screen--and it's delivered without a chime).

Share more than photos - previously, you could share photos; in the new iOS you can share memories--so if you have a group of photos from that amazing trip to Boring Town, USA, you can share them with all of your friends.

If you want the big giant list of everything new in iOS 12, visit: https://www.apple.com/ios/ios-12/features/

THANKS FOR THE NICE GESTURE, APPLE!

And now the moment you've been reading for: how to make your way around an iPad Pro without the button.

Remember, these gestures are pretty universal--they work on the iPad Pro and they work on iPhones that don't have the Home button.

HOME

First, the easiest gesture: getting to your Home screen. Do you have your pen and paper ready? It's complicated.... swipe up from the bottom of your screen. That's it. It's not too far off from pushing a button. Heck, your fingers even in the same place! The only difference is your moving your thumb upward instead of inward.

MULTITASK

As Dorothy would say, there's no place like Home--but we can still give a shoutout to multitask, can't we? If you don't know what it is, multitask is how you switch quickly between apps--you're in iMessage and want to open up Safari to get a website, for example; instead of closing iMessage, finding Safari from the Home screen, and then repeating the process to get back, you use multitask to do it quickly.

On the old iPad's you would double press the Home button. On the new iPad Pro, you Swipe Up from the bottom as if you were going to home...but don't lift your finger; instead of lifting your finger, continue swiping up until you reach the middle of your screen--at this point, you should see the multitask interface.

If you have an app open (Note: this does not work on the Home screen), you can also slide your finger right across the bottom edge of the screen; this will go to the previous app open.

MISSION CONTROL

If you haven't noticed, I'm putting these features in other of use. So, the third most common gesture people use is the Control Center. That's where all your Controls are located--go figure...Control is where controls are!

We'll go over Control panel closer later in the book. For now, just know that this where you'll do things like adjust brightness, enable airplane mode, and turn on the beloved flashlight. On the old iPad, you accessed Control Center by swiping up from the bottom of the screen. No Bueno on the new iPad Pro--if you recall, swiping up gets you Home.

To new gesture for Control Center is swiping down from the upper right corner of the iPad Pro (not the top middle, which will do something else).

NOTIFICATIONS

Eck! So many gestures to remember! Let me throw you a bone. To see notifications (those are the alerts like email and text that you get on your tablet and phone), swipe down from the middle of the screen. That's the same way you did it before! Finally, nothing new to remember!

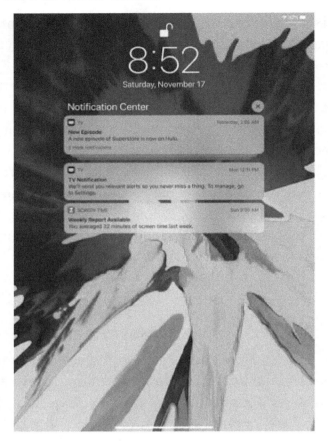

I hate to steal your bone back, but about not remembering anything: there is something to remember. :-(

If you swipe down from the right corner, you get the Control Center; that wasn't the case on old iPad. Swiping down anywhere on top got you to the home screen. On the new iPad Pro, you can only swipe in the middle.

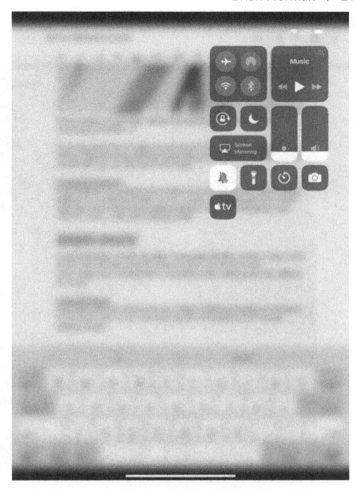

SEARCHING FOR ANSWERS

If you're like me, you probably have a million apps--and because you want to see the wallpaper on your iPad Pros Home screen, you put those million apps in one folder! That may not be the best way to organize a library, but the search function on the iPad Pro, makes it easy to find anything quickly.

In addition to apps, you can use search to find calendar dates, contacts, things on the Internet. The best part of search? Works the same way it does on older iPads...there's your bone back! From your Home screen, swipe down in the middle of the screen.

WIDGETS

Many apps come with what's known as a Widget. Widgets are basically mini versions of your favorite app--so you can see the weather, for example, without actually opening the app.

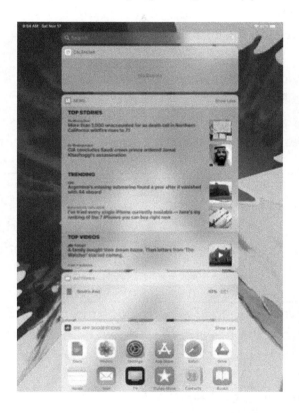

The gesture to see widgets is the same on the new iPad Pro as the old. Hurray! Something else you don't have to learn. From the Home or Lock screen, swipe right and they'll come out.

RECAP

Okay, so you only got a minute to get up and running, and you need the 1-minute summary of everything important?

Let's cover gestures. The right side will be the way the gesture used to work, and left side will be the way it works on new iPad Pros.

Previous Generation iPad Pro	Next Generation iPad Pro
Go to the Home screen - Press the Home button.	Go to the Home screen - Swipe up from the bottom of your screen.
Multitask - Double press Home button.	Multitask - Swipe up from the bottom of your screen, but don't lift your finger until it reaches the middle of the screen.
Control Center - Swipe up from the bottom of the screen.	Control Center - Swipe down from the upper right corner of the iPad Pro.
Notifications - Swipe down from the top of the screen.	Notifications - Swipe down from the middle top of the screen.
Search - From the Home screen, swipe down from the middle of your screen.	Search - From the Home screen, swipe down from the middle of your screen.

Access Widgets - From the Home or Lock screen, swipe right.	Access Widgets - From the Home or Lock screen, swipe right.

[2]

IPAD PRO VS. IPAD VS. COMPUTER

This chapter will cover:
- What's so special about Pro models and do you need it?
- Do you still need a computer

When iPad first burst on the scene in 2010, there was one; there were no different sizes, different speeds, different resolutions. Times have changed. There are all kinds of different iPads now, and five different sizes: iPad Pro 12.9", iPad Pro 11", iPad Pro 10.5", iPad 9.7", iPad Mini

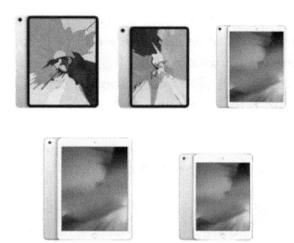

So, what's the difference between all of the iPad stack up? First the obvious:

The iPad Pro is nearly 13 inches; the iPad (previously the largest iPad) is just shy of 10, and iPad Mini 2 is almost 8 inches.

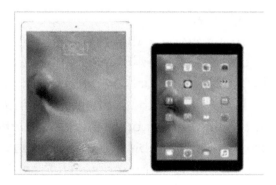

In terms of thickness, the iPad Mini 4 is surprisingly larger than the newest iPad Pro (the Pro is 5.7mm and the Mini is 6.1), but realistically, you probably wouldn't be able to tell which one is the thickest unless they were side by side. What you will notice is the weight; the iPad Pro is nearly double the weight of the Mini (468 grams and 298.8 grams, respectively--that's about 1 pound and a little more than half a pound). When you are carrying it in a backpack, it's obviously going to be a welcome relief from a larger laptop but holding it for long periods at a time could be a bit cumbersome for some.

Battery life is the same across all devices (app. 10 hours). So are the cameras (the iPad Pro's back camera does have better resolution 12MP then non-pros--they also record video in 4K); the newest Pro also has the live photos feature that's found on newer iPhones but not 3D touch; all the newest model iPad's, however, do have fingerprint IDs. Storage starts at 64GB on the Pros and goes up to 1TB.

All of the iPads have HD screens; the most pixels per inch is found on the iPad Mini, which has 326 PPI; both the larger iPad Pros have 264 PPI.

So far, they sound pretty much the same. It's really under the hood that you start seeing a difference; the iPad Pro is built much like higher end notebooks. It has a 64-bit processor and A12 chip. To give an example of how powerful that is in more basic terms—the Macbook that Apple began selling in 2015 has been recorded as being slower than the thin little tablet.

Why do you need that much power? If you do a lot of graphic editing, then you'll be thankful you bought the larger model. The iPad Pro is powerful enough to edit 4K video seamlessly.

The iPad Pro line is also the only Apple tablet compatible with the new Apple Pencil, which, for artist is really a game changer.

So, who is the iPad Pro best for? Students who want a hybrid computer (i.e. one with a detachable) keyboard, graphic artist / videographers who want to edit their work on the go, or people who want to ditch their computers altogether.

How does it stack up against other devices (notably it's biggest competitor in the hybrid tablet category: The Windows Surface)? In terms of speed, it's comparable. The tradeoff is you cannot install popular Windows app, nor is there any SD slot--the newest Pros, however, have USB-C. But iPads have always been known for their cutting-edge apps—something you simply will not find on the Windows app store.

COMPUTER OR IPAD?

Can an iPad really replace a computer? That really depends. An iPad Mini and iPad Air are ideally more casual products—perfect for when you just want to browse the Internet or check email. The iPad Pro is the first Apple tablet that really stands a chance of replacing your computer.

In terms of Apple products (not counting Apple's desktop line: Mac Mini, iMac, and Mac Pro), there's basically four products to consider: iPad

Pro, MacBook Air, MacBook, and MacBook Pro. Let's look at who is best for each one:

iPad Pro: Great for students, artist, and commuters who want a lightweight tablet with computer-like speeds. For some users, the advantage will also be it's almost the same operating system as the iPhone, so if you know your way around an iPhone, then this will be easy for you.

MacBook Air: The MacBook Air is a terrific lightweight alternative; the biggest trade-off with the MacBook Air used to be graphics, but the latest model fixed this with Retina displays.

MacBook: MacBook was updated in 2015; it looks great—but looks can be deceiving. As it has been pointed out, the iPad Pro (which is cheaper) has outperformed it in many tests. It's great for portability but is lacking if you have heavy tasks you need to do.

MacBook Pro: The MacBook Pro is Apple's best laptop; it's fast, and still relatively light. It's the best laptop you can buy, but if you aren't using graphic intensive programs, then you probably don't need the best.

Can the iPad replace a computer? For some people, yes. But you'll want to make sure you load up on the right accessories (like a comfortable keyboard), which can make the iPad less portable and even as heavy as a laptop.

[3]

STARTING UP

This chapter will cover:
- Setup
- Common gestures and terminology
- The Keyboard

SETTING UP

I don't want to take away from the main topics to spend several pages setting up your iPad Pro. The setup is straightforward, and the onscreen help gives you everything you need to know. There are a few things, however, you should know about the setup:

You can change things. If you say yes (or no) to something but change your mind, you'll be able to change it in the Settings, which I will walk you through in corresponding sections throughout this book.

If you are moving from an older iPad to the iPad Pro and want to keep all of the settings, make sure and back it up before restoring it over the cloud. To do this, go into "Settings". Next, click your account name (first thing you'll see on top). Then "iCloud" and "iCloud Backup" (near the middle when you scroll), and finally "Back Up Now".

Face ID - Face ID is probably new to you unless you have last year's iPhone X. One thing that's worth pointing out is you can add multiple faces. For example, if your spouse or child uses your tablet, they can add their face to Face ID and won't have to put in a passcode or ask you to unlock it everytime they want to use it.

While the iPad Pro box does not contain a manual, there is a manual available online. You can access it here: https://support.apple.com/manuals/ipad

Gestures

Throughout the book, I'll refer to certain gestures. To make sure you understand the terminology, below are the most common ones:

Tap

This is the "click" of the iPad world. A tap is just a brief touch. It doesn't have to be hard or last very long. You'll tap icons, hyperlinks, form choices, and more. You'll also tap numbers on a touch keypad in order to make calls. It's not exactly rocket science, is it!

TAP AND HOLD

This simply means touching the screen and leaving your finger in contact with the glass. It's useful for bringing up context menus or other options in some apps.

DOUBLE TAP

This refers to two rapid taps, like double clicking with your finger. Double tapping will perform different functions in different apps. It will also zoom in on pictures or webpages.

3D TOUCH: PRESS

I actually won't refer to this gesture. Why? Because it doesn't exist on the iPad Pro. I'm pointing it out because if you are an iPhone user, you might be wondering if you are doing something wrong-- it's a very common iPhone gesture.

SWIPE

Swiping means putting your finger on the surface of your screen and dragging it to a certain point and then removing your finger from the surface. You'll use this motion to navigate through menu levels in your apps, through pages in Safari, and more. It'll become second nature overnight, I promise.

DRAG

This is mechanically the same as swiping, but with a different purpose. You'll touch an object to select it, and then drag it to wherever it needs to go and release it. It's just like dragging and dropping with a mouse, but it skips the middleman.

PINCH

Take two fingers, place them on the iPad Pro screen, and move them either toward each other or away from each other in a pinching or reverse pinching motion. Moving your fingers together will zoom in inside many apps, including web browsers and photo viewers; moving them apart will zoom out.

ROTATE AND TILT

Many apps on iPad Pro take advantage of rotating and tilting the device itself. For instance, in the paid app Star Walk, you can tilt the screen so that it's pointed at whatever section of the night sky you're interested in – Star Walk will reveal the constellations based on the direction the iPad Pro is pointed.

Emoji's

The reason you shelled out $100s for an iPad Pro that's more powerful than many computers was to send out adorable emojis in your text messages, right? Okay...maybe not! Your grandkids will be pretty impressed if you send them to them, I bet.

The keyboard, and by extension Emoji's, is something you do a lot with your iPad, so it's worth learning more about it before digging deeper into the software that relies on them.

Anytime you type a message, the keyboard pops up automatically. There are no extra steps. But there are a few things you can do with the keyboard to make it more personal.

There are a few things to notice on the keyboard – the delete key is marked with a little x (it's right next to the letter M), and the shift key is the key with the upward arrow (next to the letter Z).

By default, the first letter you type will be capitalized. You can tell what case the letters are in though at a quick glance.

To use the shift key, just tap it and then tap the letter you want to capitalize or the alternate punctuation you'd like to use. Alternatively, you can touch the shift key and drag your finger to the letter you want to capitalize. Double tap the shift key to enter caps lock (i.e. everything is capitalized) and tap once to exit caps lock.

SPECIAL CHARACTERS

To type special characters, just tap and hold the key of the associated letter until options pop up. Drag your finger to the character you want to use and be on your way. What exactly would you use this for? Let's say you're are writing something in Spanish and need the accent on the "e"; tapping and holding on the "e" will bring that option up.

USING DICTATION

Let's face it: typing on the keyboard stinks sometimes! Wouldn't be easier to just say what you want to write? If that sounds like you, then Dictation can help! Just tap the microphone next to the spacebar and start talking. It works pretty well.

NUMBER AND SYMBOL KEYBOARDS

Of course, there's more to life than letters and exclamation marks. If you need to use numbers, tap the 123 key in the bottom left corner. This will bring up a different keyboard with numbers and punctuation.

From this keyboard, you can get back to the alphabet by tapping the ABC key in the bottom left corner. You can also access an additional keyboard which includes the remaining standard symbols by tapping the #+- key, just above the ABC key.

EMOJI KEYBOARD

And finally, the moment you've waited for! Emojis!

The emoji keyboard is accessible using the smiley face key between the 123 key and the dictation key. Emojis are tiny cartoon images that you can use to liven up your text messages or other written output. This goes far beyond the colon-based emoticons of yesteryear - there are enough emojis on your iPad Pro to create an entire visual vocabulary.

To use the emoji keyboard, note that there are categories along the bottom (and that the globe icon on the far left will return you to the world of language). Within those categories, there are several screens of pictographs to choose from. Many of the human emojis include multicultural variations. Just press and hold them to reveal other options.

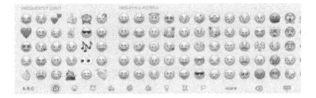

Multilingual Typing

Most people are probably all set. They know all they need to know about typing on the iPhone and they're ready to blast emoji's at their friends. There are a few other features that apply to some (not all people)

One such feature is Multilingual Typing. This is for people who type multiple languages at the same time. So, if you type between Spanish and English, you won't keep seeing a message saying your spelling is wrong.

If that sounds like you, then you just need to enable another dictionary, which is simple. Go to Settings > General > Dictionary.

Configuring International Keyboards

If you find yourself typing in a different language fairly often, you may want to set up international keyboards. To set up international keyboards, visit Settings > General > Keyboard > Keyboards. You can then add an appropriate international keyboard by tapping Add New Keyboard. As an example, iPad Pro has great support for Chinese text entry – choose from pinyin, stroke, zhuyin, and handwriting, where you actually sketch out the character yourself.

When you enable another keyboard, the smiley emoji key will change to a globe icon. To use international keyboards, tap the Globe key to cycle through your keyboard choices.

Your iPad Pro is loaded with features to help prevent slip-ups, including Apple's battle-tested autocorrect feature, which guards against common typos. In iOS 8, Apple introduced a predictive text feature that predicts what words you're most likely to type, and its accuracy is even better in the new iOS.

Three choices appear just above the keyboard – the entry as typed, plus two best guesses. Predictive text is somewhat context-specific, too. It learns your speech patterns as you email your boss or text your best friend, and it will serve up appropriate suggestions based on who you're messaging or emailing. Of course, if it bothers you, you can turn it off by visiting Settings > General > Keyboards and turning off predictive text by sliding the green slider to the left.

[4]

THE BASICS

This chapter will cover:
- Home Screen
- Making Calls
- Adding and removing apps
- Sending messages
- iMessage Apps
- Notifications
- AirDrop
- Multitasking

HOME

There's one thing that has pretty much stayed the same since the very first iPad was released: The Home screen. The look has evolved (and the Dock on the bottom has changed a little), but the layout has not. All you need to know about it is it's the main screen. So, when you read me say "go to the

Home screen" this is the screen I'm talking about. Make sense?

THE DOCK

The dock is the bottom portion of your home screen.

This is where you can "dock" the apps you love and use the most. If you've used an older iPad or iPhone, then I'm sure you know all about it. But this dock is a little different.

Look at the above screenshot. Now look to the right. See that line? If not, look at the one below:

The apps to the right of that line are not put there by you. These are the last three apps you've used. So, these will always be changing. It helps you multitask much quicker.

MAKING CALLS

Your iPad Pro is a great phone.

You read that right! In addition to thousands of other things, your iPad Pro can make phone calls. It does this two ways:

Over wi-fi with FaceTime Audio

With your iPhone

There are a number of ways you can make calls:

- If you are on a website or map and there's a phone number with a hyperlink, that means you can tap it and it will dial the number. Note: to do this, you have to have an iPhone tethered to your iPad Pro. The call will come from your iPhone's phone number.

- If someone sends you an iMessage on your iPad (we'll cover iMessage later in this chapter), you can tap that name and tap FaceTime Audio; the call will be made using FaceTime Audio.

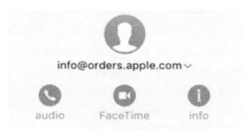

- The Contacts app has a list of all your contacts (hence the apps name!); any contact who has an iPhone that's tied to the given email will have a FaceTime Audio option--or, if your iPhone is tethered to your iPad Pro, an option to dial them directly.

Receiving a call is fairly intuitive. If your iPad Pro is tied to your iPhone, and the phone is in range of the iPad Pro, then the call will come to your iPad Pro as well. Swipe to answer. That's it.

THERE'S AN APP FOR THAT

App is short for application. So, when you hear the term "There's an app for that." It just means there's a program that does what you want to do. If you're a Windows use, all those things you always open (like Word and Excel) are apps. Apple has literally millions of apps. Opening an app is as simple as touching it.

Unlike apps on a computer, you don't have to close apps on your phone. It's all automatic. For most apps, it will even remember where you were so when you open it again, it's saved.

ORGANIZING APPS

If you're like me--and pretty much most people are--you love your apps and you have a lot of them! So, you'll need to know how to move them around, put them in folders, and delete them. It's all easy to do.

The Home screen may be the first screen you see, but if you swipe to the right, you'll see there's more. Personally, I keep the most used apps on the first screen, and not so used apps in folders on the second. The bottom dock is where I put the apps I use all the time (like mail and Safari).

To rearrange apps, take your finger and touch one of your apps and hold it there until the icon giggles. When the apps are jiggling like that, you can touch them without opening them and drag them around your screen. Try it out! Just touch an app and drag your finger to move it. When you've found the perfect spot, lift your finger and the app drops into place. After you've downloaded more apps, you can also drag apps across home screens.

You can delete an app using the same method for moving them. The only difference is instead of moving them, you tap the X in the upper left corner of the icon. Don't worry about deleting something on accident. Apps are stored in the cloud. You can delete and install them as many times as you want; you don't have to pay again--you just have to download them again.

Putting apps on different screens is helpful, but to be really organized you want to use folders. You can, for example, have a folder for all your game apps, finance apps, social apps. Whatever you want. You pick what to name it. If you want a "Apps I use on the toilet" folder, then you can absolutely have it!

To create a folder, just drag one app over another app you'd like to add into that folder.

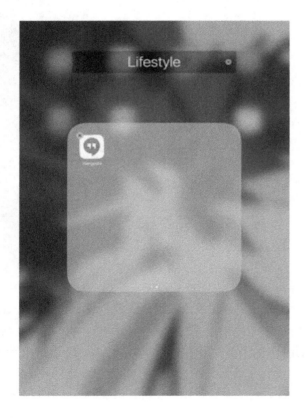

Once they are together, you can name the folder. To delete the folder, just put the folder apps in "jiggle mode" and drag them out of the folder. iPad Pro doesn't allow empty folders – when a folder is empty, iPad Pro deletes it automatically.

MESSAGING

More and more tablet users are staying connected through text messages instead of phone calls, and the iPad Pro makes it easy to keep in touch with everyone. You can also use iMessage to interact with other Apple users. This feature allows you to send instant messages to anyone signed into a Mac running OS X Mountain Lion or higher, or any iOS device running iOS 5 or greater. iMessage for iOS 11 has been completely changed to make everything just a little more...animated.

On the main Messages screen, you will be able to see the many different conversations you have going on. You can also delete conversations by swiping from right to left on the conversation you'd like and tapping the red delete button. New conversations or existing conversations with new messages will be highlighted with a big blue dot next to it, and the Message icon will have a badge displaying the number of unread messages you have, similar to the Mail and iPad Pro icons.

To create a message, click on the Messages icon, then the Compose button in the top right corner.

Once the new message dialog box pops up, click on the plus icon to choose from your contacts list, or just type in the phone number of the person you wish to text. For group messages, just keep adding as many people as you'd like. Finally, click on the bottom field to begin typing your message.

iMessage has added in a lot of new features over the past few years. If all you want to do is send a message, then just tap the blue up arrow.

But you can do so much more than just send a message! (Please note, if you are sending a message with newer features to someone with an older OS or a non-Apple device, then it won't look as it appears on your screen).

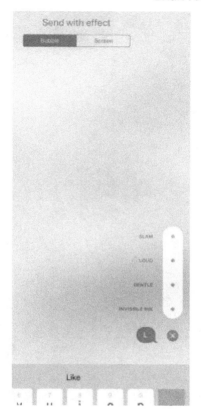

On the top of this screen, you'll also notice two tabs; one says "Bubble" and the other says "Screen"; if you tap "Screen" you can add animations to the entire screen. Swipe right and left to see each new animation.

When you get a message that you like, and you want to respond to it, you can tap and hold your finger over the message or image; this will bring up different ways you can react.

Once you make your choice, the person on the receiving end will see how you responded.

If you'd like to add animation, a photo, a video, or lots of other things, then let's look at the options next to the message.

You have three choices--which bring up even more choices! The first is the camera, which let's you send photos with your message (or take new photos--note, these photos won't be saved on your iPad Pro), the next let's you used iMessage Apps (more on that in a second), and the last let's you record a message with your voice.

Let's look at the camera option first.

New Feature Alert! You can now add stickers, text, effects and more when you send someone a photo.

If you want to take an original photo, then tap the round button on the bottom. To add effects, tap the star in the lower left corner.

Tapping effects brings up all the different effects available to you. I'll talk more about Animoji soon but as an example, this app lets you put an Animoji over your face (see the example below--not bad for an author photo, eh?!)

Finally, the last option is apps. You should know all about iPad Pro apps by now, but now there's a new set of apps called iMessage apps. These apps let you be both silly (send digital stickers) or serious (send cash to someone via text). To get started, tap the plus sign to open the message app store.

You can browse all the apps just like you would the regular app store. Installing them is the same as well.

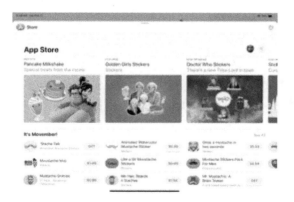

When you're ready to use the app, just tap apps, tap the app you want to load, and tap what you want to send. You can also drag stickers on top of messages. Just tap, hold and drag.

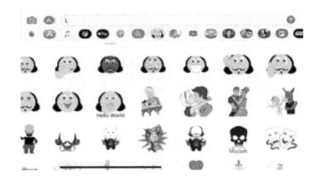

Also, in the app section is a button called #images.

If you tap on this button you can search for thousands of humorous meme's and animated GIFs. Just tap it and search a term you want to find—such as "Money" or "Fight".

One final iMessage feature worth trying out is the personal handwritten note. Tap on a new message like you are going to start typing a new message; now rotate your tablet horizontal. This brings up an option to use your finger to create a handwritten note. Sign away, and then hit done when you're finished.

NOTIFICATIONS

When you have your tablet is locked, you'll start seeing notifications at some point; this tells you things like "You have a new email", "Don't forget to set your alarm", etc.

New Feature Alert: Notifications can get overwhelming if you don't open your iPad Pro to clear them. iOS 12 introduced Grouping to notifications.

So, when you see all your notifications on you lock screen, they'll be organized by what they are. To see all the notifications from any one category, just tap it.

Not a fan of Grouping? No problem. You can turn it off for any app. Head to Settings, then Notifications, then tap the app you want to turn grouping off for. Under Notification Groupings, just turn off automatic.

USING AIRDROP

AirDrop was introduced in iOS 7, though Apple fans have likely used the Mac OS version on MacBooks and iMacs. In Mac OSX Sierra and Yosemite, you'll finally be able to share between iOS and your Mac using AirDrop.

AirDrop is Apple's file sharing service, and it comes standard on iOS 12 devices. You can activate AirDrop from the Share icon anywhere in iOS 12. If other AirDrop users are nearby, you'll see anything they're sharing in AirDrop, and they can see anything you share.

MULTITASKING

Multitasking has been on the iPad Pro since its release, but because many people are upgrading to iPad Pro from iPads, it's going to be a new feature for most.

There're three kinds of such multitasking:

Slide Over: (available on iPad Air, iPad Pro, iPad Air 2, iPad mini 2, iPad mini 3, and iPad mini 4) If you're working in one app, you can swipe from the right side of the screen to view and work with a second app; swipe down to pick a different app.

This option is mainly if you want to check something quickly, but don't want to have the app running next to it.

Below is what Slide Over looks like running Maps:

Split View: (iPad Pro, iPad Air 2 and iPad mini 4) To keep to apps open at the same time, tap the app divider and drag it; this locks it onto the screen. Drag the divider to resize the app pane. To close it, slide the divider all the way to the right of the screen; this same method also lets you switch the app. This feature is supported on all Apple apps, but for other apps, it's up to the developer to include it. So, if you don't see a divider you can adjust, it just means the developer has not included this feature.

Picture in Picture: (iPad Air, iPad Air 2, iPad mini 2, iPad mini 3, and iPad mini 4) As a video plays (or during a FaceTime video call), press the Home button and the video scales down to a corner of your display. You can also pinch it with three fingers to shrink it.

Once it's shrunk, you can move it around your screen to any of the four corners.

If you want to close the video, tap the "X"; if you want to enlarge it, tap the far-left button; and if you want to play it within another app, just open any app. Below you can see it running within Safari.

[5]

A LITTLE MORE THAN BASIC

This chapter will cover:
- Sending Email
- Surfing the Web
- Using iTunes
- Apple Music
- Finding Apps on the App Store
- Adding Calendar Items
- Using Maps
- Find My Friends
- Find My Phone
- Notes

MAIL

The iPad Pro lets you add multiple email addresses from virtually any email client you can think of. Yahoo, Gmail, AOL, Exchange, Hotmail, and many more can be added to your iPad Pro so that you will be able to check your email no matter where you are. To add an email address, click on the Settings app icon, then scroll to the middle where you'll see Mail, Contacts & Calendar. You will then see logos for the biggest email providers, but if you have another type of email just click on "Other" and continue.

If you don't know your email settings, you will need to visit the Mail Settings Lookup page on the Apple website. There you can type in your entire email address, and the website will show you what information to type and where in order to get your email account working on the tablet. The settings change with everyone, so what works for one provider may not work with another. Once you are finished adding as many email accounts as you may need, you will be able to click on the Mail app icon on your tablet's home screen and view each inbox separately, or all at once.

SURFING THE INTERNET WITH SAFARI

You've already seen how the address bar works. To search for something, you use the same exact box. That's how you can search for anything on the Internet. Think of it like a Google, Bing, or Yahoo! search engine in the corner of your screen. In fact, that's exactly what it is. Because when you search, it will use one of those search engines to find results.

On the bottom of the screen you'll see five buttons; the first two are back and forward buttons that makes the website go either backwards or forwards to the website you were previously on.

Next to the address bar, is a button that lets you share a website, add it to the 'Home Screen', print it, bookmark it, copy it, or add it to your reading list.

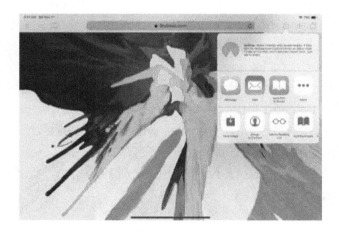

That's great! But what does it all mean? Let's look at each button on the menu:

Social Buttons: Mail, Message, Twitter, Facebook are 'Social Buttons'; pressing any of them will share the website you are looking at with whichever button you pressed (Message, FYI, is text message)

Add to Home Screen: If you go to a website frequently, this can be very convenient. What this button does is add an icon for that webpage right to your 'Home screen'. That way whenever you want to launch the website, you can do it directly from the 'Home screen'.

Print: If you have an AirPrint compatible printer, you can print a photo, document or webpage directly from your tablet.

Copy: This copies the website address.

Bookmark: If you go to a website often but don't want to add it to your 'Home screen' then you can bookmark it. I will show you this in more detail in just a moment.

Add to Reading List: If you have a bunch of news stories open, you can add them to a Reading List to read later (even if you are offline).

The next button over, which looks like a book, is the bookmark button.

Let's go back to the bookmark button and see how that works.

When you add a bookmark (remember you do this from the previous button, the middle one), it will ask you to name it. By default, it will put it in the general bookmarks tab, but you can also create new folders by clicking on 'Bookmarks'.

Now you can access the website anytime you want without typing the address by tapping on the Bookmarks button.

The iCloud tab is something you'll want to pay attention to if you use another Apple device (like an iPad, an iPod Touch or a Mac computer). Your safari browsing is automatically synced; so, if you are browsing a page on your iPad, you can pick up where you left off on your iPad Pro.

The last button looks like a box on top of a transparent box.

If you use a computer or an iPad; then you probably know all about tabs. Apple decided to not use tabs on 'Safari'. Tabs are there in another way though, that's what this button is; it lets you have several windows open at the same time. When you press it, a new window appears. There's an option to open a New Page. Additionally, you can toggle between the pages that you already have opened. Hitting the red 'x' will also close a page that you have opened. Hit done to go back to normal browsing.

When you put your tablet in landscape (i.e. you turn it sideways), the browser also turns, and you will now have the option to use Full-Screen mode. Tap the double arrows to activate it.

Reading list is the middle icon that looks like a pair of glasses where you can view all of the web pages, blog posts, or articles that you've saved for offline reading. To save a piece of internet litera-ture to your reading list, tap on the Share icon and then click on Add to Reading List. Saved pages can be deleted like a text message by swiping from right to left and tapping on the red Delete button.

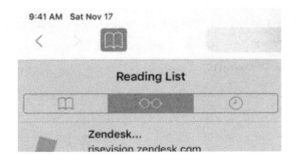

The third tab on the Bookmarks page is where you can view your shared links and subscriptions. Subscriptions can be created from any web page that provides RSS feeds, and your tablet will automatically download the latest articles and posts. To subscribe to a site's RSS, visit the website, tap the Bookmark icon, and select Add to Shared Links.

Back on the main Safari home page, the last button found on the bottom right corner is Tabs. Just like the Mac version you can have multiple tabs of web pages open at the same time, and switch between them with ease. To switch the tabs into private mode where your browsing history or cookies will not be saved or recorded, tap the Tabs button and select Private. You will be asked to either close all existing tabs or keep them. If you don't want to lose any tabs that might still be open, opt to keep them. Existing tabs, in addition to any new tabs you open, will now be shielded behind private browsing.

ITUNES

The iTunes app found on your home screen opens the biggest digital music store in the world. You will be able to purchase and download not just music, but also countless movies, TV shows, audiobooks, and more. On the iTunes home page, you can also find a What's Hot section, collections of music, and new releases.

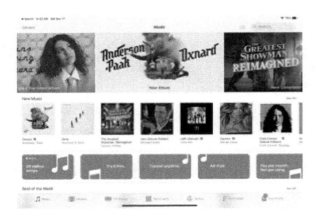

At the top, you will see the option to view either featured media or browse through the top charts. On the upper left corner is the Genres button. Clicking Genres will bring up many different types of music to help refine your search.

New Feature Alert: When you search a lyric in iTunes, it now brings back results.

APPLE MUSIC

Apple Music is a relatively new service from Apple that gives you the ability to stream the entire iTunes store and receive curated playlists from music experts tailored to your preferences. It costs $9.99 a month, but you can take advantage of the three-month free trial to see if this service is for you before paying for it. It also offers discount subscription pricing for family plans and college students.

BUYING APPS

So how do you buy, download and finally remove apps? I'll look at that in this section.

To purchase apps, and I don't actually mean paying for them because you can buy a free app without paying for it, follow the following:

The first thing you see when you open the app store are the feature apps. This is to say games, lots and lots of games! Games are the top telling category in the app store, but don't worry, there is more there than just games. Later in this hand-book, I will tell you some of the essential apps you should get, but for now, let's see how the app store works so that you discover some of them yourself.

If you hear about a new app and want to check it out, use the 'Search' option.

Q Search

When you find an app you want to buy, simply tap the price button and type in your App store password. Remember that just because an app is free to download doesn't mean you won't have to pay something to use it. Many apps use 'in-app purchases' which means that you have to buy something within the app. You will be notified be-fore you purchase anything though.

Apps are constantly coming out with updates like new, better features. Updates are almost al-ways free, unless noted, and are easy to install. Just click on the last tab: 'updates'. If you have any apps that need to be updated, you will see it here. You will also see what's new in the app. If you see one, tap 'update' to begin the update.

If you bought an app, but accidentally deleted it, or changed your mind about deleting it, don't worry! You can download the app again in the same place that you see the updates. Just tap on 'Purchased'.

When you tap the 'Purchased' button, you will see two options: one is to see all the apps you have purchased and one to just see the apps that you have purchased but are not on your iPad Pro. Tap the one that says 'Not on This iPad to re-download anything, at no cost. Just tap the Cloud button to the right of the screen. You can even download it again if you bought it on another iPad as long as it's under the same account.

Deleting apps is easy; on your 'home' screen, tap and hold the icon of the app you want to remove, then tap the 'x' on top of the app.

CALENDAR

Among the other pre-installed apps that came with your new iPad Pro, perhaps one of the most used apps you'll encounter is the calendar. You can switch between viewing appointments, tasks, or everything laid out in a one day, one week, or one-month view.

Combine your calendar with email accounts or iCloud to keep your appointments and tasks synced across all of your devices, and never miss another appointment.

CREATING AN APPOINTMENT

To create an appointment, click on the Calendar icon on your home screen. Click on whichever day you would like to set the appointment for, and then tap the plus sign (+) in the corner. Here you will be able to name and edit your event, as well as connect it to an email or iCloud account in order to allow for syncing.

When editing your event, pay special attention to the duration of your event. Select the start and end times, or choose "All Day" if it's an all-day event. You will also have a chance to set it as a recurring event by clicking on Repeat and selecting how often you want it to repeat. In the case of a bill or car payment, for example, you could either select Monthly (on this day) or every 30 days, which are two different things. After you select your repetition, you can also choose how long you'd like for that event to repeat itself: for just one month, a year, forever, and everything in between.

MAPS

The Maps app is back and better than ever. After Apple parted ways with Google Maps several years ago, Apple decided to develop its own, made-for-iPad map and navigation system. The result is a beautiful travel guide that takes full advantage of the newest iPad Pro resolutions. Full screen mode allows every corner of the tablet to be filled with the app, and there's an automatic night mode. You'll be able to search for places, restaurants, gas stations, concert halls, and other venues near you at any time, and turn-by-turn navigation is available for walking, biking, driving, or commuting. Traffic is updated in real time, so if an accident occurs ahead of you or there is construction going on, Maps will offer a faster alternative and warn you of the potential traffic jam.

The turn-by-turn navigation is easy to understand without being distracting, and the 3D view makes potentially difficult scenarios (like highway exits that come up abruptly) much more pleasant.

Another convenient feature is the ability to avoid highways and toll roads entirely.

To set up navigation, tap on the Maps icon. On the bottom of the screen is a search for place or address; for homes you need an address, but businesses just need a name. Click on it and enter your destination once prompted.

When you find your destination's address, click on Route, and choose between walking or driving directions. For businesses, you also have the option of reading reviews and calling the company directly.

For hands-free navigation, press and hold the home button to enable Siri (which will be discussed in the next section) and say "Navigate to" or "Take me to" followed by the address or name of the location that you'd like to go to.

If you'd like to avoid highways or tolls, simply tap the more options button and select the option that you want.

Apple Maps also lets you see a 3D view of thousands of locations. To enable this option, tap the "i" in the upper right corner. After this, select satellite view.

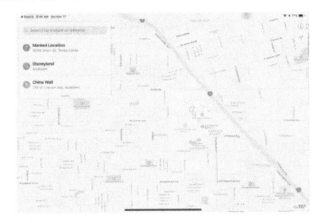

If 3D view is available, you'll notice a change immediately. You can use two fingers to make your map more or less flat. You can also select 2D to remove 3D altogether.

FIND MY FRIENDS

Find My Friends is a social people finder app that can also be run as a widget in your Notifications center. The app displays a map that shows exactly where your friends are and how far away they are from you. You'll have to add friends using the Add function in the top right corner, and your friends will have to approve the service. You can even set up notifications that alert you when a friend leaves or arrives at a specified location by tapping a friend's icon in the app and then tapping Notify Me.

FIND IPHONE

Find iPhone is a useful app that allows you to see the location of all of your Apple devices on a map. You can remotely play sounds on devices (to help you find them under a pile of laundry, for example), send messages to them, and remotely erase them in case of theft. Of course, the app that's installed on your iPhone won't help you find your iPhone, but if your phone goes missing and you don't have any other Apple devices, just log on to icloud.com to see where your device has wandered to.

NOTES

The Notes app has always been the go-to app for jotting down quick and simple notes—it's like Word or Pages, but without all the fancy stuff. In iOS 9, Notes is still simple—but it got a whole lot fancier...while retaining the simplicity that people love about it.

At first glance, Notes looks basically the same as it always has. Notice that little plus sign above the keyboard? That's what's different.

Tap the plus button one time, and you'll see the options that have been added.

Starting from the left side is a checkmark, which is what you press if you'd like to make a checklist instead of a note. For each new checkmark, just tap the return button the keyboard.

○ Check list
○ Item 2
○ Item 3|

The "Aa" button is what you would press if you would like to format the note a little (larger fonts, bold, bulleted text, etc.).

Formatting   Done

тιue

Heading

Body   ✓

● Bulleted List

─ Dashed List

The little camera button will let you add a photo you have taken or let you take a photo from within the app and insert it.

Photo Library

Take Photo or Video

Cancel

And finally, the squiggly line lets you draw in the Notes app; when you press it, you'll see three different brushes (pen, marker, and pencil) that each work a little differently, as well as a ruler and eraser.

There's also a round black circle—tapping that lets you change the color of the brush.

Just tap the Done button in the upper right corner once you've picked your color and it will be changed.

Once you tap the Done button after you've finished drawing, you will go back to the note. If you tap the drawing, however, it will activate it again and you can make changes or add to your drawing.

It's obviously not the most advance drawing app—but that's the point—it's not supposed to be. As the name of the app says, this app is just for jotting or drawing quick notes.

In the Settings menu a Search option has been added at the top. There's a lot of Settings in iOS and there's more and more with each update—search settings let you quickly access the setting you want. So, for instance, if you want to stop getting notifications for a certain app, you no longer have to thumb through endless apps—now just search for it.

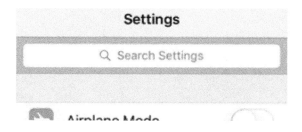

Notes has also been added to Safari, so if you want to add a website to a note, it's now possible.

[6]
CUSTOMIZING

This chapter will cover:
- Screen Time
- Do Not Disturb Mode
- Notifications and Widgets
- General Settings
- Sounds
- Customizing Brightness and Wallpaper
- Adding Facebook, Twitter and Flickr Accounts
- Family Sharing
- Continuity and Handoff

Now that you know your way around, it's time to dig into the settings and make this tablet completely custom to you!

For most of this chapter, I'll be hanging out in the Settings area, so if you aren't already there, tap Settings from your Home screen.

SCREEN TIME

New Feature Alert:
Screen Time lets you see just how much time you spend on your tablet, and doing what. You may be surprised--heck, you may not even want to know about this feature! You can also use it to monitor the amount of time you kids spend on their devices.

To use Screen Time, head on into Settings > Screen Time

According to the image above, I've been on my tablet 41 minutes; that's not too bad...but I've only had my tablet on for 42!

You can click on any app to see how much time you've spent in it, and even what your average is. From here you can also add limits.

DO NOT DISTURB MODE

Do Not Disturb mode is a handy feature located near the top of your Settings app. When this operational mode is enabled, you won't receive any notifications and all of your calls will be silenced. This is a useful trick for those times when you can't afford to be distracted (and let's face it, your iPad Pro is as communicative as they come, and sometimes you'll need to have some peace and quiet!). Clock alarms will still sound.

To turn on, schedule and customize Do Not Disturb, just tap on Do Not Disturb in Settings. You can schedule automatic times to activate this feature, like your work hours, for example. You can also specify certain callers who should be allowed when your tablet is set to Do Not Disturb. This way, your mother can still get through, but you won't have to hear every incoming email. To do this, use the Allow Call From command in Do Not Disturb settings.

Do Not Disturb is also accessible through the Control Center (swipe up from the bottom of the screen to access it at any time).

NOTIFICATIONS AND WIDGETS

Notifications are one of the most useful features on the iPad Pro, but chances are you won't need to be informed of every single event that's set as a default in your Notifications Center. To adjust Notifications preferences, go to Settings > Notifications.

By tapping the app, you can turn Notifications off or on and finesse the type of notification from each app. It's a good idea to whittle this list down to the apps that you truly want to be notified from

– for example, if you're not an investor, turn off Stocks! Reducing the number of sounds your iPad Pro makes can also reduce tablet-related frazzledness. For example, in Mail, you may want your tablet to make a sound when you receive email from someone on your VIP list but to only display badges for other, less important email.

General Settings

The General menu item is a little bit of a catchall. This is where you'll find information about your iPad Pro, including its current version of iOS and any available software updates. Fortunately, iOS 12 ushers in an era of smaller, more efficient updates, so you won't find yourself scrambling to delete apps in order to make space for the latest improvements. You can also check your tablet and iCloud storage here.

The Accessibility options are located here as well. You can set your iPad Pro according to your needs with Zoom, Voiceover, large text, color adjustment, and more. There are a quite a few Accessibility options that can make iOS 12 easy for everyone to use, including Grayscale View and improved Zoom options.

A handy Accessibility option that's a little disguised is the Assistive Touch setting. This gives you a menu that helps you access device-level functions. Enabling it brings up a floating menu designed to help users who have difficulty with screen gestures like swiping or with manipulating the iPad Pro's physical buttons. Another feature for those with visual needs is Magnifier. Turning this on allows your camera to magnify things, and you can also click the home button and magnify anything that you're looking at.

I'll cover this more at the end of the book.

SOUNDS

Hate that vibration when your tablet rings? Want to change your ring tone? Head to the Sounds Settings menu! Here you can turn vibration on or off and assign ring tones to a number of iPad Pro functions. We do suggest finding an isolated space before you start trying out all the different sound settings – it's fun, but possibly a major annoyance to those unlucky enough not to be playing with their own new iPad Pro!

Tip: You can apply individual ringtones and message alerts to your contacts. Just go to the person's contact screen in Contacts, tap Edit, and tap Assign Ringtone.

CUSTOMIZING BRIGHTNESS AND WALLPAPER

On the iPad Pro, wallpaper refers to the background image on your home screen and to the image displayed when your iPad Pro is locked (lock screen). You can change either image using two methods.

For the first method, visit Settings > Wallpapers. You'll see a preview of your current wallpaper and lock screen here. Tap Choose a New Wallpaper. From there, you can choose a pre-loaded dynamic (moving) or still image, or choose one of your own photos. Once you've chosen an image, you'll see a preview of the image as a lock screen. Here, you can turn off Perspective Zoom, which makes the image appear to shift as you tilt your tablet) if you like. Tap Set to continue. Then choose whether to set the image as the lock screen, home screen, or both.

The other way to make the change is through your Photo app. Find the photo you'd like to set as a wallpaper image and tap the Share button. You'll be given a choice to set an image as a background, a lock screen, or both.

If you want to use images from the web, it's fairly easy. Just press and hold the image until the Save Image / Copy / Cancel message comes up. Saving the image will save it to your Recently Added photos in the Photos app.

PRIVACY

The Privacy heading in Settings lets you know what apps are doing with your data. Every app you've allowed to use Location Services will show up under Location Services (and you can toggle Location Services off and on for individual apps or for your whole device here as well). You can also go through your apps to check what information each one is receiving and transmitting.

Mail, Contacts, Calendars Settings

If you need to add additional mail, contacts or calendar accounts, tap Settings > Mail, Contacts and Calendars to do so. It's more or less the same process as adding a new account in-app. You can also adjust other settings here, including your email signature for each linked account. This is also a good place to check which aspects of each account are linked – for example, you may want to link your Tasks, Calendars and Mail from Exchange, but not your Contacts. You can manage all of this here.

There are a number of other useful settings here, including the frequency you want your accounts to check for mail (Push, the default, being the hardest on your battery life). You can also turn on features like Ask Before Deleting and adjust the day of the week you'd like your calendar to start on.

Adding Facebook and Twitter

If you use Twitter, Facebook or Flickr, you'll probably want to integrate them with your iPad Pro. This is a snap to do. Just tap on Settings and look for Twitter, Facebook and Flickr in the main menu (you can also integrate Vimeo and Weibo accounts if you have them). Tap on the platform you want to integrate. From there, you'll enter your user name and password. Doing this will allow you to share webpages, photos, notes, App Store pages, music and more straight from your iPad Pro's native apps.

iPad Pro will ask you if you'd like to download the free Facebook, Twitter and Flickr apps when you configure your accounts if you haven't already done so. We recommend doing this – the apps are easy to use, free, and look great.

We found that when we associated our Facebook accounts, our contact list got extremely bloated. If you don't want to include your Facebook friends in your contacts list, adjust the list of applications that can access your Contacts in Settings > Facebook.

FAMILY SHARING

Family Sharing is one of our favorite iOS 12 features. Family Sharing allows you to share App Store and iTunes purchases with family members (previously, accomplishing this required a tricky and not-entirely-in-compliance-with-terms-of-service dance). Turning on Family Sharing also creates a shared family calendar, photo album, and reminder list. Family members can also see each other's location in Apple's free Find My Friends app and check the location of each other's devices in the free Find iPhone app. Overall, Family Sharing is a great way to keep everyone entertained and in sync! You can include up to six people in Family Sharing.

To enable Family Sharing, go to Settings > iCloud. Here, tap Set Up Family Sharing to get started. The person who initiates Family Sharing for a family is known as the family organizer. It's an important role, since every purchase made by family members will be made using the family organizer's credit card! Once you set up your family, they'll also be able to download your past purchases, including music, movies, books, and apps.

Invite your family members to join Family Sharing by entering their Apple IDs. As a parent, you can create Apple IDs for your children with parental consent. When you create a new child Apple ID, it is automatically added to Family Sharing.

There are two types of accounts in Family Sharing – adult and child. As you'd expect, child accounts have more potential restrictions than adult accounts do. Of special interest is the Ask to Buy option. This prevents younger family members from running up the family organizer's credit card bill by requiring parental authorization for purchases. The family organizer can also designate other adults in the family as capable of authorizing purchases on children's devices.

If you'd like to further lock down your children's iOS devices, be sure to take a look at 5.2 for information about setting up additional restrictions!

CONTINUITY AND HANDOFF

iOS 12 includes some incredible features for those of us who work on multiple iOS 12 and Sierra and Yosemite OSX devices. Now, when your computer is running Yosemite or higher or your iOS 12 iPad is connected to the same Wi-Fi network as your iOS 12 iPhone, you can answer calls or send text messages (both iMessages and regular SMS messages) from your iPad or computer.

The Handoff feature is present in apps like Numbers, Safari, Mail and many more. Handoff allows you to leave an app in one device mid-action and pick up right where you left off on a different device. It makes life much easier for those of us living a multi-gadget lifestyle.

[7]
THE CAMERA

This chapter will cover:
- Taking photos and videos
- Editing photos
- Sharing photos and videos

TAKING PHOTOS AND VIDEOS

Now that you know how to make a tablet call, let's get back to the fun stuff! I'll look at using the photo app next.

The camera app is on your 'Home' screen, but you can also access it from your 'lock' screen for quick, easy access.

The camera app is pretty simple to use. First, you should know that the camera app has two cameras; one on the front and one on the back.

The front camera has a lower resolution and is mostly used for self-portraits; it still takes excellent photos, but just remember the back camera is better. To access it, tap the button in the top right corner (the one with the camera and two arrows). The bar on the bottom has all your camera modes. This is how you can switch from photo to video mode.

On the side of the screen you will see a lightening button. That's your flash. Tap this button and you can toggle between different flash modes.

The next two buttons you won't use quite as much. The first, the circle, is for live photos; live photos takes a short video while you take the photo; it's so quick you won't even know it did it; it's on automatically, so tap it once to turn it off; if you tap and hold a photo with live photo enabled, then you will see the video. Next to that is a timer, which, as you might expect, delays the shot so you can take a group photo.

One of the photo modes is called "Pano" or Panorama. Panorama is the ability to take an extra long photo that's over 20 megapixels in size. To use it tap the 'Panorama' button. On screen instructions will now appear. Simply press the 'Shoot' button at the bottom of the screen, and rotate the camera as straight as possible while following the line. When it reaches the end, the photo will automatically go into your album.

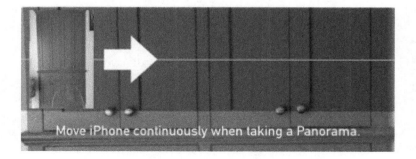

Move iPhone continuously when taking a Panorama.

The mode you've probably seen the most about is Portrait Mode. Portrait Mode gives your photos that blurred effect you see on high-end DSLR cameras.

Whether a user is a selfie lover or a photo portrait addict, these are two features all users will appreciate.

To access and use portrait mode and portrait light mode on the iPad Pro:

Bring up the camera app.

Swipe up or down to switch to the Portrait setting.

Line up the shot within 2-8 feet of the subject. The camera's face and body detection will automatically identify the subject and provide instruction to move further or get closer to the subject.

Pay attention to the Camera app's prompts: More light required, flash may help, place subject within 8 feet, or move farther away.

When the shot is ready a banner will appear at the bottom.

Swipe or tap on the cube icons above the shutter button to change lighting effects.

Press the shutter button to take the photo.

Note: Users can still shoot with the telephoto lens in Portrait mode even if the banners don't turn yellow — it just means a lesser depth or lighting effect.

There's several different Portrait Modes (studio lighting, for example), but you can switch modes after you take the photo; so, if you take it with Studio Lighting, but decide another mode would look better, then you can change it.

New Feature Alert: The newest iPad Pros can now adjust the depth of the blur after the photo is taken. To do this, just select Edit after the shot is taken. This only works for photos taken with Portrait Mode.

PHOTO EDITING

Editing your photos is just as easy as taking them. As simple as editing tools are, they are also quite powerful. If you want more power though, you can always download one of the hundreds of photo editing apps in the app store.

To edit a photo, tap the 'Photo' icon on your 'Home' screen.

When you launch 'Photos', you will see a tab with three buttons; right now, I'll be talking about the 'Photos button, but we'll talk about 'Photo Stream' in the next chapter. Tap albums and let's get editing!

Next, tap the photo you want to edit and then tap 'edit' in the upper-right corner. This will open the editing menu. On the bottom of the screen, you will see all the options: undo, auto correct (which corrects the color of the photo), color change, red eye removal, and finally crop.

The only added feature is the middle one, which let's you change the color saturation.

When you are satisfied with the changes tap save in the upper right corner.

Remember whenever you want to get to the previous screen just tap the back button in the upper-left corner.

EDITING LIVE PHOTOS

Apple introduced Live Photos in 2015, when the iPhone 6s came out. This feature enhances the tablets photography, using pictures that move. iOS 12 makes Live Photos better than ever. Wanna know how to take a live photo? Let's have a look.

Live Photos records what happens 1.5 seconds before and after you take the photo. That means you're not only getting a photo, you're also getting movement and sound.

Open the Camera app

Set your camera to photo mode, and turn Live Photos on

Hold the tablet very still

Tap .

With your iPad Pro, Live Photos is naturally on by default. If you want to take a still image, tap and you'll be allowed to turn off Live Photos. If you want Live Photos to always be off, go to Settings > Camera > Preserve Settings.

PHOTO ALBUMS AND PHOTO SHARING

So now that your photo is taken and edited, let's see how to share photos.

There are several ways to share photos. When you open a photo, you will see an option bar on the bottom. The older version had more options— these options have now been moved to one central place, which you will see next.

The first button lets you share the photo socially and to media devices.

The top row is more of the social options; the bottom row is more of the media options. AirPlay, for example, let's you wirelessly send the photos if you have an Apple TV.

Finally, the last button lets you delete the photo, don't worry about accidently deleting a photo, because it asks you to confirm if you want to delete the photo before you delete it.

Next, let's go to the middle tab. 'Photo Stream' is sort of like 'Flickr'; it lets you share your photos with your family and friends easily. To get 'Photo Stream', tap the 'Shared button on the bottom of the photo app.

On the top left corner is a '+' sign; tap it.

This brings up a menu that lets you create a shared directory. From there you can choose the name, who sees it and if it's a public or private photo stream. To choose a person in your contacts tap the blue '+' sign.

Once the album is created, tap the plus sign and tap on each photo you want to add, then hit done.

Once your family or friend accepts your 'Stream' invitation, you will automatically begin syncing your photos. Anytime you add a photo to your album, they will receive a notification.

The new iOS will now also group your photos as memories; it does this by looking at where the photo was taken and when it was taken. So, you'll start noticing groups like "Christmas Memories."

Now that you know your way around, it's time to dig into the settings and make this tablet completely custom to you!

For most of this chapter, I'll be hanging out in the Settings area, so if you aren't already there, tap Settings from your Home screen.

[8]

ANIMOJI

This chapter will cover:
- What is Animoji
- How To Use Animoji

HOW TO ADD YOUR OWN ANIMOJI

I'm going to be honest, I think Animoji--even creepy! What is it? You almost have to try it to understand it. In a nutshell, Animoji turns you into an emoji. Want to send someone an emoji of a monkey? That's fun. But you know else is fun? Making that monkey have the same expression as you!

When you use Animoji, you put the camera in front of you. If you put out your tongue, the emoji sticks out it's tongue. If you wink, the emoji winks.

So, it's a way to send a person an emoji with exactly how you are feeling.

To use it, open your iMessage app. Start a text the way you normally would. Tap the App button followed by the Animoji button. Choose an Animoji and tap to see full screen. Look directly into the camera and place your face into the fame. Tab the record button and speak for up to 10 seconds. Tap the preview button to look at the Animoji. Tap the upward arrow button to send or the trashcan to delete.

You can also create an emoji that looks like you. Click that big plus sign next to the other animoji's.

This will walk you through all the steps to send your very own custom animoji--from hair color to type of nose.

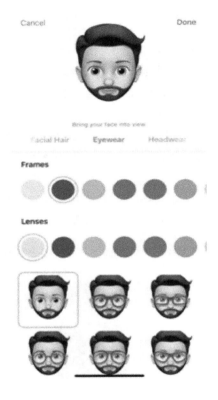

When you're done, you are ready to send.

[9]

SIRI

This chapter will cover:
- Siri

By now, you probably know all about Siri and how it can remind you of things. If not, say "Hey, Siri"

So, what exactly do you do with it? The first thing you should do is introduce Siri to your family. Siri is pretty smart, and she wants to meet your family. To introduce her to your family, activate Siri and say: "Brian is my brother" or "Susan is my boss." Once you confirm the relationship you can now say things like: "Call my brother" or "email my boss."

Siri is also location-based. What does that mean? It means that instead of saying: "Remind me to call wife at 8 am" you can say: "Remind me when I leave work to call wife" and as soon as you step out of the office you will receive a reminder. Siri can be a bit frustrating at first, but it's one of the tablet's most powerful apps, so give it a chance!

Everyone hates dealing with waits. There's nothing worse than being hungry and having to wait an hour for a table. Siri does her best to make your life easier by making reservations for you. For this to work, you'll need a free app called 'Open-Table' (you'll also need a free account), which is in the 'Apple App store'. This app makes its money by restaurants paying it, so don't worry about having to pay to use it. Once it's installed, you will simply activate Siri (press the Home button until it turns on) and say: "Siri, make me a reservation at the Olive Garden", (or wherever you want to eat). Note that not all restaurants participate in 'Open-Table', but hundreds (if not thousands) do, and it's growing monthly, so if it's not there, it probably will be soon.

Siri is ever evolving. And with the latest update, Apple has taught her everything she needs to know about sports. Go ahead, try it! Press and hold the 'Home' button to activate Siri, and then say something like: "What's the score in the Kings game" or: "Who leads the league in homeruns?"

Siri has also got a little wiser in movies. You can say: "Movies directed by Peter Jackson" and it will give you a list and let you see a synopsis, the review rating from 'Rotten Tomatoes', and in some cases even a trailer or an option to buy the movie. You can also say: "Movie show times" and a little of nearby movies playing will appear. At this time, you cannot buy tickets to the movie, though one can imagine that option will be coming very soon.

Finally, Siri, can open apps for you. If you want to open an app, simply say: "Open and the apps name."

The new iOS lets you add shortcuts to Siri; you can see this in Settings > Siri & Search > Shortcuts.

[10]

ACCESSIBILITY

This chapter will cover:
- Accessibility features

When it comes to accessibility on the iPad, there's a lot you can do. To simplify things, I'll break it up into four short sections:

- Vision
- Interaction
- Hearing
- Media & Learning

This will make it easier to skip whatever isn't relevant to you.

Before I get to any of that, where exactly do you find Accessibility? What's great about Apple products is you find things almost the same on any Apple device--which means the way we find accessibility here is the same way you find it on Apple Watch and iPhone.

So where is it?!

First, tap the "Settings" icon.

Next, go to "General."

And finally, tap on "Accessibility."

Accessibility   >

VISION

Vision accessibility features take up more than any other feature. If you're sitting there thinking, "I can see just fine" I'd still recommend checking out

this second. There's more hear than just seeing--
you may see perfectly fine, but still, prefer text a
little larger or bolder.

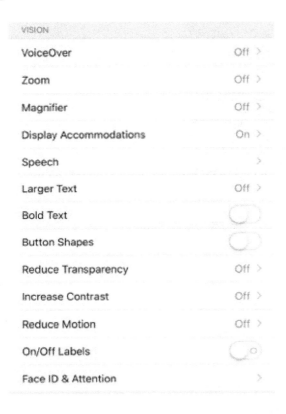

I'm going to go through the list of accessibility
features you should know about below, and, if nec-
essary, how to use it. Some will be pretty self-
explanatory.

First up: VoiceOver. To access it, just tap
VoiceOver.

> ‹ Accessibility   **VoiceOver**
>
> **VoiceOver**
>
> VoiceOver speaks items on the screen:
> - Tap once to select an item
> - Double-tap to activate the selected item
> - Swipe three fingers to scroll
> - To go Home: Slide one finger up from the bottom edge until you feel the first vibration and lift your finger
> - To use the App Switcher: Slide up farther from the bottom until you feel a second vibration and lift your finger
> - To use Control Center: Slide one finger down from the top edge until you feel the first vibration and lift your finger
> - To use Notification Center: Slide down farther from the top until you feel a second vibration and lift your finger
>
> SPEAKING RATE
>
> Speech   ›
>
> Verbosity   ›
>
> Braille   ›
>
> Audio   ›
>
> Rotor   ›
>
> Rotor Actions   ›
>
> Typing Style   Standard Typing   ›

VoiceOver reads everything that happens on your screen. What do I mean everything? Exactly that! If you adjust the volume up, then VoiceOver will say back to you that the volume has turned up.

Turning this on is simple: flick the toggle. Controlling this feature? Not quite as simple. Turning it on means several of the normal gestures on the iPad are changed a little.

To go home, for example, you swipe up until you feel a vibration; if you want to switch apps, you swipe up a little further until you feel a second vibration.

The person reading things back is probably a little too fast by default. To slow him down a bit, use the slider under "Speaker Rate." The closer to the turtle icon you get, the slower it will be.

If you like VoiceOver, but don't like how long it takes for him to read something back, you can make him a little less wordy by tapping on Verbosity.

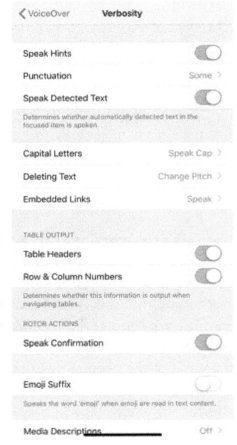

Braille is an interesting feature on the iPhone. You can't exactly feel braille on your phone after all. So how does it work? To use it, you need a braille reader that connects to your phone (usually via Bluetooth).

‹ VoiceOver	**Braille**	
Output	Eight-dot ›	
Input	Six-dot ›	
Braille Screen Input	Six-dot ›	
Status Cells	›	
Equations use Nemeth Code		
Show Onscreen Keyboard		
Turn Pages when Panning		
Word Wrap		
Braille Code	English (Unified) ›	
Alert Display Duration	3s ›	
CHOOSE A BRAILLE DISPLAY...		
Searching...		

What else about VoiceOver do you need to know? The features under Braille will be a little less commonly used. Rotor controls actions you'll take to receive VoiceOver; Always Speak Notifications toggled on will read back any message you get automatically.

If you decide to use this feature, there's a number of third-party apps that are built for it. Just a few: TapTapSee, Seeing AI, Voice Dream Writer, Read2Go.

Below VoiceOver is Zoom. Zoom is a bit less intrusive than VoiceOver; it turns on only when you tap the assigned gesture, so you might forget that it's even on.

Once you toggle Zoom on, you can activate it at any time by double tapping with three fingers. Take note there: three fingers! Use one finger and this isn't going to happen--three fingers have to touch the screen. To exit zoom, repeat this.

At the bottom of the screen, there's a slider to adjust the zoom level; by default, it's 5x; you can go up to 15x.

By default, when you tap with three fingers, you'll get a small zoomed in window; want to see the entire screen? Go to Zoom Region, and select Full Screen Zoom.

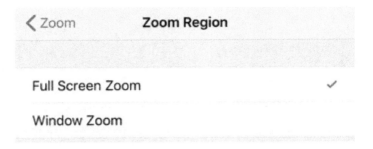

If your phone is in color, but when you zoom, you want it in greyscale--or any other filter--you can change that in Zoom Filter.

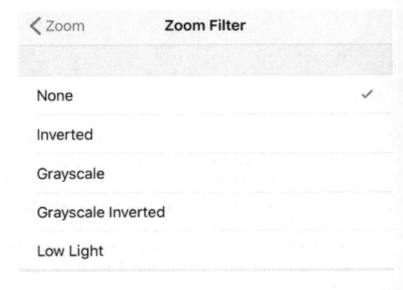

Below Zoom is a handy little feature called "Magnifier."

When you switch the toggle to on, a shortcut is added to use your phone as a magnifying glass. Tripple-click the side button and a magnify app opens up.

Near the bottom of the screen is a slider to adjust the zoom.

Display Accommodations is where you can make your screen black and white--or a number of different settings. Just go into Display Accommodations, select Color Filters, toggle Color Filters to on, and select your color scheme.

In Display Accommodations, you can also reduce the intensity of bright colors, turn off auto brightness, and invert colors.

One of the most common accessibility features is Larger Text; when turned on, this increases the font size for all compatible apps. On the bottom of this feature is a slider--adjust it to the right to make the font bigger, and two the left to make it smaller.

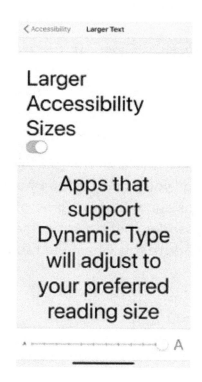

Finally, reduce motion makes the interface a little less--motion-y! What do I mean? The easiest way to explain this is for you to go to your Home screen. Move your phone around. See how the icons and background appear to be moving? If that annoys you or makes you dizzy, then toggle this on to turn it off.

< Accessibility   **Reduce Motion**

Reduce Motion

Reduce the motion of the user interface, including the parallax effect of icons.

INTERACTION

Interaction is the area that pertains to gestures and the things you touch on the phone to launch different apps and widgets. Some of these require special accessories that do not come with your phone; it will note this when you tap on the feature.

INTERACTION

Reachability

Swipe down on the bottom edge of the screen to bring the top into reach.

Switch Control	Off >
AssistiveTouch	Off >
Touch Accommodations	Off >
Side Button	>
Siri	>
3D Touch	On >
Tap to Wake	
Keyboard	>
Shake to Undo	On >
Vibration	On >
Call Audio Routing	Automatic >

For the most part, these features will help you if you have difficulty touching the screen and find that you often open or type the wrong things as a result.

AssistiveTouch can use a special accessory, but it doesn't require one. When turned on, it turns a round shape on your screen that works a bit like a large cursor. Tapping it opens up the box below and holding it will close the app. If you really miss that home button on the phone, then you can think of it like a virtual home button--it even looks like one. Tap it once to bring up the menu and hold it to return to the home screen.

Does Siri never understand you? You aren't alone. I once asked Siri to call my wife and she tried to call John. No idea who John is or why it sounds like "wife"! If you'd rather type to Siri to prevent that kind of mishaps, you can turn it on here.

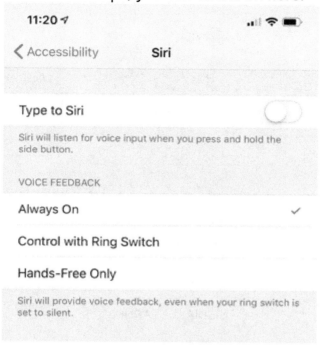

HEARING

If you are using a hearing aid with your phone, then you'll add it and make adjustments to it in this setting. If you are looking for an alternative to a hearing aid, some people use Apple's own AirPods. If you want to do this, then it's recommended that you use third-party apps such as Petralex Hearing Aid. My suggestion, if you want to try this route, is to find cheaper airplugs

HEARING

MFi Hearing Devices   >

RTT/TTY   Off >

LED Flash for Alerts   Off >

Mono Audio

Phone Noise Cancellation

Noise cancellation reduces ambient noise on phone calls
when you are holding the receiver to your ear.

L   R

Adjust the audio volume balance between left and
right channels.

Hearing Aid Compatibility

Hearing Aid Compatibility improves audio quality with some
hearing aids.

MEDIA & LEARNING

The last section is useful if you want to watch movies and TV shows with captioning or audio descriptions (i.e. it will read back the action that is happening on your screen)

MEDIA

Subtitles & Captioning >

Audio Descriptions Off >

LEARNING

Guided Access On >

Accessibility Shortcut Guided Access >

[11]

MAINTAIN AND PROTECT

This chapter will cover:
- Security
- Keychain
- iCloud
- Battery Tips

SECURITY

Passcode (dos and don'ts, tips, etc.)

In this day and age, it's important to keep your device secure. You may or may not want to set up a touch ID (you will read more about it next), but at the very least it's a good idea to maintain a passcode. Anytime your tablet is unlocked, re-started, updated, or erased, it will require a passcode before allowing entry into the tablet. To set up a passcode for your iPad Pro, go to Settings > Passcode, and click on Turn Passcode On. You will be prompted to enter a 4-digit passcode, then re-enter to confirm. Here are a few tips to follow for maximum security:

Do's

DO create a unique passcode that only you would know

DO change it every now and then to keep it unknown

DO select a passcode that can be easily modified later when it's time to change passcodes

Don'ts

DON'T use a simple passcode like 1234 or 5678

DON'T use your birthday or birth year

DON'T use a passcode someone else might have (for example, a shared debit card pin)

DON'T go right down the middle (2580) or sides (1470 or 3690)

ENCRYPTION

With all of the personal and sensitive information that can be stored on iCloud, security is understandably a very real concern. Apple agrees with this, and protects your data with high level 128-bit AES encryption. Keychain, which you will learn about next, uses 256-bit AES encryption - the same level of encryption used by all of the top banks who need high levels of security for their data. According to Apple, the only things not protected with encryption through iCloud is mail (because email clients already provide their own security) and iTunes in the Cloud, since music does not contain any personal information.

KEYCHAIN

Have you logged onto a website for the first time in ages and forgot what kind of password you used? This happens to everyone; some websites require special characters or phrases, while others require small 8-character passwords. iCloud comes with a highly encrypted feature called Keychain that allows you to store passwords and login information in one place. Any of your Apple devices synced with the same iCloud account will be able to load the data from Keychain without any additional steps.

To activate and start using Keychain, simply click on Settings > iCloud and toggle Keychain on, then follow the prompts. After you've added accounts and passwords to Keychain, your Safari browser will automatically fill in fields while you remain logged into iCloud. If you are ready to checkout after doing some online shopping, for example, the credit card information will automatically pre-fill, so you don't have to enter any sensitive information at all.

ICLOUD

To really get the full effect of Apple's carefully created ecosystem and be a part of it, you will need to create an iCloud account. Simply put, iCloud is a powerful cloud system that will seamlessly coordinate all of your important devices. The cloud can be a little difficult to understand, but the best way to think about it is like a storage unit that lives in a secure part of the internet. You are allocated a certain amount of space, and you can put the things that mean the most to you here to keep safe. In the case of iCloud, Apple gives you 5 GB for free.

Your tablet lets you automatically back up certain files such as your photos, mail, contacts, calendars, reminders, and notes. In the event that your tablet is damaged beyond repair or is lost or stolen, your data will still be stored safely on iCloud. To retrieve your information, you can either log onto icloud.com on a Mac or PC, or log into your iCloud account on another iPad Pro to load the information onto that tablet.

With the introduction of iOS 8 and the iPhone 6 and 6 Plus, Apple rolled out a few major changes. You will now be able to store even more types of documents using iCloud Drive and access them from any smartphone, tablet, or computer. Additionally, up to 6 family members will now be able to share purchases from iTunes, and the App Store, removing the need to buy an app twice simply because you and a loved one have two different iCloud accounts.

For users who will need more than 5 GB, Apple has dramatically reduced the cost of iCloud:

50 GB is $0.99 per month

200 GB is $2.99 per month
1 TB (1000 GB) is $9.99 per month
2 TB (2000 GB) is $19.99 per month

BATTERY TIPS

The iPad Pro promises amazing battery life. But let's face it, no matter how great the battery is, you probably would love to have just a little bit more life in your charge.

DISABLE NOTIFICATIONS

My mom told me her battery didn't seem to be lasting very long. I looked at her tablet and could not believe how many notifications were activated. She knows absolutely nothing about stocks, nor does she have any desire to learn, and yet she had stock tickers going. You might want notifications on something like Facebook, but there are probably dozens of notifications running in the background that you don't even know about, nor do you even need to. Getting rid of them is easy; Go to 'Settings', then to 'Notifications'. Anything that shows up as 'In Notification Center' is currently active on your tablet. To disable them, tap on the app and then switch it to off. They aren't gone for good; anytime you want to turn them back on, just go to the very bottom where it says, 'Not In Notification Center' and switch them back on.

BRIGHTNESS

Turning down the brightness just a shade can do wonders for your tablet and might even give your eyes some needed relief. It's easy to do; Go to 'Settings', then to 'brightness'. Just move the slider to a 'setting' that you feel comfortable with.

EMAIL

I prefer to know when I get email as soon as it comes. By doing this, my tablet is constantly re-freshing email to see if anything has come in; this drains the battery, but not too terribly. If you are the kind of person who doesn't really care when they get email, then it might be good to just switch it from automatic to manual. That way it only checks email when you tap the mail button. To switch manual on, go to 'Settings', then to 'Mail, Contacts, Calendars' and finally go to 'Fetch New Data'. Now go to the bottom and tap 'Manually' (you can always switch it back later).

LOCATION, LOCATION, LO…BATTERY HOG

Have you heard of location-based apps? These apps use your location to determine where you are exactly. It's actually a great feature if you are using a map of some sort. So, let's say you are looking for somewhere to eat and you have an app that recommends restaurants, it uses your GPS to de-termine your location, so it can tell what's nearby.

That is great for some apps, but it is not so for others. Anytime you use GPS, it's going to drain your battery, so it's a good idea to see what apps are using it and question if you really want them to. Additionally, you can turn it off completely and switch it on only when needed. To do either, go to 'Settings', then to 'Location Services', switch any app you don't want to use this service to off (you can always switch it back on later).

Accessorize

90% of you will probably be completely content with these fixes and happy with their battery life; but if you still want more, consider buying a batter pack. Battery packs do make your tablet a bit bulkier (they slide on and attach to the back of your tablet), but they also give you several more hours of life. They cost around $70. Additionally, you can get an external battery charger to slip in your purse or briefcase These packs let you charge any USB-C device. External battery chargers cost about the same, the one advantage of a charger versus' a pack is it will charge any device that has a USB-C, not just the iPad Pro.

The easiest way to save battery life, however, is to go to Settings > Battery and switch on "Low Power Mode". This is not the ideal setting for normal tablet use, but if you only have 20% of your battery and need it to last longer, then it's there.

APPENDIX A: ACCESSORIES

APPLE PENCIL

The biggest companion to the iPad Pro—perhaps the reason you bought the device—is the Apple Pencil. The Pencil looks like a normal stylus, but it's much more sophisticated then that; there's actually a tiny processor inside of it and when you use it, it's scanning for a signal over 240 times a second.

Unlike other stylus', the Apple Pencil has a battery built into it. To charge it, simply connect it to the magnetic side of the ipad. Apple says you can get 30 minutes of life into the Pencil by charging it for just 15 seconds. Don't worry about constantly charging it, however—it will last roughly 12 hours.

Using the Apple Pencil is also easy; as soon as you touch the Pencil to your screen, the iPad can sense that it's a Pencil and not a finger; pressing the Pencil harder on the iPad will make the line or object you are drawing darker; pressing it softer will make it lighter. If you want to add shading, tilt the Pencil; the sensors inside the Pencil calculate the orientation and angle of your hand.

SMART KEYBOARD FOR IPAD PRO

The keyboard is full-size--meaning it's the same size and spacing you are used to on larger tablets. Being full-size means there's room for shortcuts.

Holding down on the CMD button next to the space bar, for example, while you are in pages, brings up the menu below:

Bold	⌘ B
Italic	⌘ I
Underline	⌘ U
Copy Style	⌘ option C
Add Comment	⌘ shift K
Find	⌘ F
Hide Word Count	⌘ shift W
Hide Ruler	⌘ R
Create Document	⌘ N

If the keyboard isn't sturdy enough for you, another keyboard to check out is the Logitech Create keyboard; it's about 10 dollars cheaper that the Apple keyboard, but works the same way. The Logitech keyboard has a backlit (so you can see the keys in the dark) and chargers through the iPad, so there's no need for batteries. It comes at a cost, however--it's about a pound in weight.

APPENDIX B: KEYBOARD SHORTCUTS

The iPad Pro shares one more thing in common with the Macbook: keyboard shortcuts. Because the keyboard has a command key, you'll be able to use the same shortcuts you may already know. Below is a list of them (note: these shortcuts will not work with every program).

- Command-X – Cuts or removes selected text or item and copies it to the clipboard.
- Command-C – Copies the selected text or item to the clipboard.
- Command-V – Pastes the contents of the clipboard into the document, app, or finder.
- Command-Z – Undoes the previous command.
- Command- Shift-Z – Redoes the previous undo.
- Command-A – Selects all text or items in the running program.

- Command-F – Opens the Find window to find documents or other items.
- Command-G – Finds the next occurrence of a previously found item (i.e. Find Again).
- Command-H – Hides the current running program or front window (Note: this will not work if you have a program running in full screen).
- Command-N – Opens a new document or window.
- Command-O – Opens an item (for instance if you are in Word or Pages and you want to open a previously saved document).
- Command-S – Save the current document.
- Command-Q – Quit an app.
- Command-Tab – Switch to the next open app (Note: if you don't let go of Command and continue hitting the Tab button, you can continue going to the next app.

DOCUMENT SHORTCUTS

The following shortcuts are applicable to supported document software like Word, PowerPoint, Pages, Excel, OpenOffice, etc.

- Command-B – Bold or un-bold the selected text.
- Command-I – Italicize or un-italics selected text.
- Command-U – Underline or remove underline to selected text.

CPSIA information can be obtained
at www.ICGtesting.com
Printed in the USA
LVHW051503130219
607426LV00015B/930/P